CHIPMUNKS

Amy-Jane Beer

Grolier
an imprint of

www.scholastic.com/librarypublishing

Published 2008 by Grolier
An imprint of Scholastic Library Publishing
Old Sherman Turnpike, Danbury,
Connecticut 06816

For The Brown Reference Group plc
Project Editor: Jolyon Goddard
Copy-editors: Lesley Ellis, Lisa Hughes,
    Wendy Horobin
Picture Researcher: Clare Newman
Designers: Jeni Child, Lynne Ross,
    Sarah Williams
Managing Editor: Bridget Giles

Volume ISBN-13: 978-0-7172-6252-6
Volume ISBN-10: 0-7172-6252-9

**Library of Congress
Cataloging-in-Publication Data**

Nature's children. Set 2.
    p. cm.
    Includes bibliographical references and
index.
    ISBN-13: 978-0-7172-8081-0
    ISBN-10: 0-7172-8081-0
    1. Animals--Encyclopedias, Juvenile. 1.
    Grolier (Firm)
    QL49.N383 2007
    590--dc22
                        2007026928

Printed and bound in China

PICTURE CREDITS

Front Cover: **Nature PL**: Aflo.

Back Cover: **Nature PL**: Aflo; **Still
Pictures**: W. Layer; **Superstock**: Age
Fotostock, George Ostertag.

FLPA: S., D., and K. Maslowski 22, 30;
Photolibrary.com: 14, Breck P. Kent 34;
Shutterstock: Robin Arnold 9, Doug Baines
21, Tanik Chavin 46, Brad Denoon 2–3, 37,
Sebastien Gauthier 6, Maxim Kazitor 33, John
Kirinic 5, 26–27, Larsek 13, Hway Kiong Lim
17, Bruce MacQueen 10, Margaret M.
Stewart 4, 45; **Still Pictures**: G. Kopp 41, W.
Layer 42, Ed Reschke 18; **Superstock**: Age
Fotostock 29, George Ostertao 38.

Contents

FACT FILE: Chipmunks

Class	Mammals (Mammalia)
Order	Rodents (Rodentia)
Family	Squirrels (Sciuridae)
Genus	Chipmunks (*Tamias*)
Species	23 species, including *Tamius striatus*, the eastern chipmunk, and *T. sibiricus*, the Siberian chipmunk
World distribution	North America and eastern Asia
Habitat	Woods, forest, and scrub; also parks and gardens
Distinctive physical characteristics	Small, squirrel-like animals with a bushy tail and bold stripes on the back and face
Habits	Active by day; usually live alone; live and store food in burrows; often hibernate in winter
Diet	Seeds, grains, nuts, berries, buds, fungi, birds' eggs, insects, and scavenged human and livestock food

Introduction

It's difficult to look at chipmunks without smiling. With their bright eyes, twitchy nose, and striped coat, they are great fun to watch. They are always on the go—dashing up and down trees and in and out of every nook and cranny, looking for food. When they find food, they either sit up to eat using their front paws or they stuff the goodies into bulging cheek pouches and rush off again, looking funnier than ever! Have you ever wondered where they are going in such a hurry or what they do when then get there?

Chipmunks are always on the alert in case enemies are close by.

The distinctive stripes on a chipmunk's coat make this member of the squirrel family easy to identify.

Close Encounter

Chipmunks are normally very shy and timid. Most prefer to stay out of sight. But where they are used to seeing people regularly, chipmunks are often very tame. This is especially true if the chipmunks are given food, such as seeds or even picnic leftovers! That is why most people see chipmunks in parks or gardens. Chipmunks know that where there are picnickers, there is always the chance of a free meal! Next time you see a curious chipmunk begging for crumbs, take the chance to get a really good look at it.

Look for the stripes on the chipmunk's back and sides—can you count them? Usually there are five dark stripes and four pale ones. Chipmunks also have stripes on their face.

Meet the Relatives

If you look carefully at a chipmunk for a while, you probably won't be surprised to learn that they are closely related to squirrels. Chipmunks have the same bushy tail, the same rounded head, and the same amazing feet that let them scamper up and down trees. Chipmunks are also related to woodchucks, prairie dogs, and ground squirrels, all of which are also types of squirrels. Some ground squirrels look a lot like chipmunks, but they don't have stripes on their face.

All of these members of the squirrel family belong to a bigger group called **rodents**. Other animals in the rodent group are mice, rats, cavies, porcupines, and beavers. Chipmunks certainly have a big family!

The woodchuck is also a member of the squirrel family. It lives in North America.

Chipmunks might eat a lot of nuts, but they also like other foods such as birds' eggs and insects.

Grandpa Chipmunk

The squirrel family, including the great, great (and several more "greats") grandparents of today's chipmunks, has been around for more than 30 million years. When squirrels first appeared in North America they easily spread to what are now Asia, Europe, and Africa because these continents were once all joined together, unlike now.

The ancestors of chipmunks have lived in North America and Canada for a very long time. They lived on Earth when saber-toothed tigers and giant mammoths roamed the land—long before the first humans appeared. Chipmunks are an important part of nature. They help plant the seeds of trees in the great forests, and they are an important food for many other animals.

East and West

Chipmunks live almost exclusively in North America. In fact, only one species, or type, of chipmunk lives outside North America. The Siberian chipmunk makes its home in Russia and Asia. The eastern chipmunk is the largest of all chipmunk species. It lives in southeastern Canada and the eastern United States, from Newfoundland to Mississippi. There are 21 different species of chipmunks in addition to the Siberian and eastern types. They are sometimes called western chipmunks because they live in western North America.

Chipmunks live in forests and woodlands and on the edges of deserts. They prefer places with sandy soil. Loose soil is less difficult to dig than hard packed or rocky soil and it also allows rainwater to drain away easily. Good drainage means there is not much danger of chipmunk burrows getting flooded.

Like other chipmunks, the eastern chipmunk spends most of its life alone.

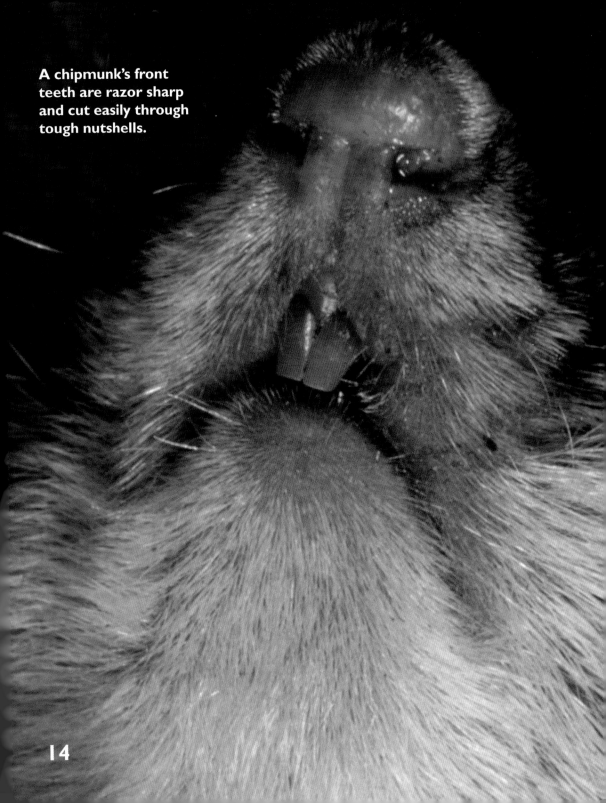

A chipmunk's front teeth are razor sharp and cut easily through tough nutshells.

Stay Sharp

Chipmunks have very long front teeth called **incisors**. They are shaped a little like chisels—a flat sharp-edged tool used to shape metal, stone, or wood. The top and bottom sets of incisor teeth rub together when the chipmunk opens and closes its mouth. This helps the teeth stay razor sharp. A chipmunk can easily open tough seeds and nut cases using its incisors. These teeth continue to grow throughout the chipmunk's life. They will never get too long because all the use wears them down.

There is a gap between the incisors and the chipmunk's other teeth. This gap lets the chipmunk close its lips behind its front teeth. So, when it is opening seeds and nuts, the chipmunk doesn't get all the bits of broken shell in its mouth.

Multipurpose Feet

Most members of the squirrel family are either great climbers or great diggers. Chipmunks have the best of both worlds. They can climb trees with great skill and ease, and are masters of burrowing. The secret of their success in both ways of life is their feet.

Chipmunk feet are large—for such a small animal—and each foot has five long fingers, or toes. Each toe has a hooked claw that is sharp enough to grip into tree bark. Chipmunk claws are also strong enough to dig without the threat of breaking. In addition, the ankle joint of each back foot can turn to face backward. That enables a chipmunk to run head first down a tree trunk.

Chipmunks are excellent tree-climbers. This skill allows them to easily escape predators that cannot climb trees.

17

A chipmunk with bulging cheek pouches watches from the entrance of its den in a tree trunk.

Chubby Cheeks

Chipmunks have front paws that look like little hands, which they can use to hold things while they sit up on their back legs. But chipmunks cannot run and hold things at the same time. When they have to carry something, they use their mouth instead. A chipmunk has very stretchy **cheek pouches**. They are dry on the inside, and the chipmunk uses them like shopping bags. It can stuff the pouches with the food it collects while it is out and about. A chipmunk can squeeze six chestnuts into its cheeks—three in each side. In fact, the cheek pouches are so stretchy that the chipmunk can fill them until they are both around the same size as the rest of its head! The chipmunk sometimes has to drop some food outside of its burrow in order to fit its cheeks through the opening.

Dig It!

Chipmunks are great diggers. They build their own homes by burrowing into the ground. A chipmunk burrow can have tunnels up to 30 feet (9 m) long, and contain one or more rooms. Digging is hard work, but for a chipmunk it is worth the effort. Burrows provide the chipmunk with a safe place to rest.

While some other burrowing squirrels have homes that look like building sites, the chipmunk goes to a lot of trouble to hide the entrance to its home. Usually the opening is tucked away at the base of a wall, a boulder, or a tree. The smart chipmunk knows that a big heap of soil outside its front door is a dead giveaway to potential **predators** looking for a tasty chipmunk dinner. As the chipmunk digs, it carries the soil out of the burrow in its cheek pouches and dumps it far away from the burrow's opening.

A chipmunk peers out from the entrance to its burrow.

An eastern chipmunk checks whether the coast is clear before leaving its burrow.

22

Summer House

Some chipmunks use the same burrow all their life and never go more than about 160 feet (50 m) from the entrance. They might make the burrow larger from time to time, by adding new rooms or entrance tunnels. Other species of chipmunks dig a fresh burrow every year. These burrows are usually simple, with just one room at the end of a tunnel.

Some forest-dwelling western chipmunks also build summer nests aboveground. These nests are made of twigs and leaves. They are usually wedged in the fork of tree branches or in hollow logs. They look like covered birds' nests, with a hole in one side and a living space inside.

Chatterboxes

Chipmunks look sweet but they are really rather grumpy little animals—at least where other chipmunks are concerned! Each adult chipmunk lives alone in its burrow. It treats the area immediately outside the burrow as its own private space, called a **territory**.

The trouble is that each chipmunk "backyard" is not large enough for the chipmunk to find everything it needs. It has to hunt farther away from its territory to find food. Trespassing on another chipmunk's territory is, therefore, unavoidable. There are often a lot of bad-tempered meetings in a chipmunk neighborhood. The chipmunk that owns the land will sit close to its burrow entrance, shouting "Chip, chip, chip!" at the top of its high-pitched, squeaky voice, until the intruder goes away. This call might explain how chipmunks got their name.

Chipmunks Beware

Chipmunks have plenty of enemies. Being active during the daytime means that chipmunks are in danger of falling **prey** to daytime hunters. All sorts of animals would be happy to have a chipmunk for dinner. These predators include foxes, raccoons, weasels, hawks, and snakes.

A chipmunk's best protection against predators are its sharp senses and its speed. Chipmunks are much more aware of their surroundings than humans are. Chipmunks have big, bright eyes high up on the sides of their head. That means chipmunks can see above them and to the sides without having to turn their head. They also have sharp hearing, which makes it difficult for any other animal to sneak up on it. At the first sign of danger, chipmunks are off—dashing for cover in a burrow or some other small place.

Like many other mammals, chipmunks have whiskers. These sensitive hairs help chipmunks feel their way around, especially in the dark.

Healthy Diet

A chipmunk's favorite diet looks like an advertisement for healthy eating. It contains seeds, nuts, and fruit—all the things we should eat plenty of, too! Fruit and grains are packed with sugar, such as starch. That gives the chipmunk all of the energy it needs for running, climbing, finding food, and fighting rivals. Seeds and nuts contain tons of **protein** for building and repairing muscles and other body parts. Seeds and nuts also contain fat, which is really important in fall. That is when the chipmunks have to put on weight in preparation for the harsh winter when food is harder to find.

Chipmunks get quite a lot of water from their food, but they need to drink every now and then, too. They sip water from pools and puddles or even from bird baths.

Even when eating,
a chipmunk keeps
a watch out for any
approaching dangers.

Chipmunks often forget where they have buried nuts. Many of these forgotten nuts grow into trees.

Treasure Trove

All the extra food a chipmunk collects over summer is stored in special larders called **caches** (KASHES). Sometimes chipmunks bury their caches in the ground or in holes in trees. But the largest caches are often stored safely inside a chipmunk's burrow.

The chipmunks' habit of storing food helped give them their official scientific name *Tamias*. The word *Tamias* means "treasurer" in Greek. A treasurer is someone that guards or looks after precious things, such as treasure or money. A chipmunk's treasure is seeds, nuts, and grains. They might not seem like riches to humans, but for a chipmunk this food can make the difference between survival or starvation in winter.

Sun Lovers

Chipmunks love to sunbathe, especially early in the morning. As they sleep underground, they can get quite chilled at night. A few minutes in the sun first thing in the morning is a great way to warm up for the day without wasting energy.

The Sun's rays are important in other ways, too. They help a chipmunk's body produce **vitamins** and other substances called **hormones**. Hormones are the body's chemical messengers.

A chipmunk's brain is very sensitive to light. The amount of sunlight a chipmunk gets each day helps its body change with the seasons. In spring, when the daylight hours are getting longer, a chipmunk's body produces hormones in preparation for breeding. Then in fall, when the days get shorter and colder, different hormones tell the chipmunk's body to start putting on weight before winter.

This chipmunk has climbed a rock to soak up the Sun's rays.

33

During hibernation, a chipmunk's breathing and heart rate slow down to save energy.

34

Sleepy Head

In winter, food is much harder to find. Staying awake and active on very cold days uses a lot of energy. Chipmunks try to save energy by staying in their burrow and sleeping a lot. They wake up every so often. If it is a warm day, they might go out, but usually it is far too cold or snowy. As long as the chipmunk has collected a good store of food, it can eat a tasty meal from its larder before going back to sleep.

Things are harder for Siberian chipmunks. Winter in Siberia is far too cold for it ever to be worth waking up, so chipmunks there don't bother. They enter a really deep sleep called **hibernation** (HI-BER-NAY-SHUN). Hibernating chipmunks use hardly any energy and can make their body fat last much longer. They don't eat at all until spring arrives.

Fattening Up

Sleeping all winter might sound like an easy option. But it is only possible if the chipmunk has put on enough extra weight in fall. The Siberian chipmunk is a champion eater! It knows which foods contain the most fats and sugars that will help build up its body stores quickest. It chooses nuts and ripe berries over fungi and other food at this time of year.

In the space of a couple of months, a Siberian chipmunk can double its body weight! But all this overeating is for a very good reason. Once it starts hibernating, a Siberian chipmunk will not eat or drink again for about six months. By the time the chipmunk wakes up, all that extra fat will have been used. The chipmunk will then need to start eating again, fast.

In fall, chipmunks
must fatten up
to survive winter.

37

A male and female chipmunk get to know each other.

Finding a Mate

Chipmunks always know when spring finally arrives. The air is warmer and the sun shines for longer each day. At this time of year, hormones produced in a chipmunk's brain cause the chipmunk to feel frisky and full of energy! One of the first things male chipmunks think about in spring is finding a mate.

As soon as a female chipmunk becomes ready to breed, all the local males start gathering on her territory. There is a lot of "chip, chip, chip" calling, plenty of scuffles and chasing about, and even some serious fights. But a female chipmunk normally likes her privacy, so having all this noise on her doorstep is quite stressful. She is only interested in the strongest and healthiest males—if any of the other males come near her, she angrily chases them away.

New Arrivals

About four to five weeks after mating, a female chipmunk gives birth to her babies. She does so in a specially prepared bed of soft grass, leaves, and downy seed heads. There are usually about four or five tiny baby chipmunks in each **litter**. Each baby weighs about one-tenth of an ounce (3 g)—less than a nickel. They have no fur and their eyes are shut tight. But their mother knows exactly how to care for them, and they grow fast. In just one month, the baby chipmunks are covered in fur and full of life. They scramble around the den and are always hungry. At first they drink their mother's milk. But by four weeks old the babies start eating solid food. By the time they are two months old, they are ready to leave home. Eastern chipmunk babies grow up so fast there is time for their mother to bring up a second litter before summer ends.

A baby chipmunk comes out of its burrow for the first time.

Once a young chipmunk
has left home, it leads
a solitary life.

Big Wide World

When young chipmunks leave home, they have a lot to learn. They are naturally cautious and alert, but many still get eaten by other animals. The first journey they make is usually only a few hundred yards. Even so, it will be the longest of their life. Once they find a place to settle, young chipmunks never stray more than about 160 feet (50 m) from their own front door. If a chipmunk is very lucky, it might live up to eight years.

Chipmunks can recognize other members of their own family by their smell. When two related chipmunks meet, they come nose to nose and sniff each other in greeting. But they don't stay together for long. They only have time for a brief meeting before they go on their way.

Keeping Clean

Chipmunks nearly always look clean and neat. That is partly because they dig their burrows in sandy soils, which hardly ever get muddy. Chipmunks also put a lot of effort into keeping their burrow clean. They throw out old bedding or food that has gone bad, for example.

Chipmunks care for their coat by bathing in dust, which sticks to any grease in their fur. They then use their claws to comb themselves. This activity is called **grooming**. The dust drops out of their fur, taking with it the grease and **parasites**, such as ticks and fleas. Chipmunks use their front paws to wipe their face and whiskers. They use their tongue and teeth to clean their feet and toes.

Chipmunks spend even more time grooming themselves when they are nervous. Scientists call this activity "displacement grooming." Humans do it, too—we fiddle with our hair or rub our face when we are anxious.

A young chipmunk
takes a break from
eating nuts to wipe
its face.

45

Chipmunks that live in parks eventually become tame enough to feed from a person's hand.

Chipmunk Mischief

Chipmunks are fun to watch, but sometimes their antics do a lot of damage. They can cause problems for gardeners and farmers by nibbling garden plants or crops and stealing seeds and grain. They also dig up newly planted seeds and snatch food put out for birds by the bulging mouthful. Their burrows can loosen the soil around fence posts or walls. Sometimes the burrows even damage the foundations of whole buildings, making them unsafe to use.

Chipmunks can become tame enough to take seeds from your hand, but you should never try to pick one up. It will not understand that you mean it no harm and its first instinct will be to bite you. With those razor-sharp front teeth, a chipmunk's bite will hurt a lot!

Index